Join Online Dating, Get Raped!

Navigating Self-Identity and the Peril of Online Relationships in the Digital Age

Index

Part I[1]

Chapter I – A New Profile

I always heard that a good book should begin by presenting the main character, so a potential reader can connect with him, or her, at an emotional level, somewhat turning the whole literary adventure into their own. What nobody ever seems to have contemplated is the problem of presenting a main character whose self-identity is actually rendered dubious by the very occurrences at hand. At first, this may seem quite unusual – we all have at least a basic idea of who we are as human beings – but how does one present a main character or a narrator who ultimately struggles with its own self-identity? Or, if you prefer, how do we even know that we know who we are?

I first confronted myself with this problem in a rather unusual way. Out of sheer boredom, and looking for truly unique people to talk to, I had just created a whole new profile in an online dating app. As it is usual in such places, I was quickly requested to submit at least one photo of myself. When I did so, I was subsequently offered the chance to verify my identity, which would supposedly ensure to other users that I was indeed myself. According to the app's information, this process would simply require me to present their staff with a new photo taken in a certain physical position. Chances are that we've all been there before, specially if you are reading this book, and the process always seems simple enough – you just take that one photo, send it to them, and shortly after you're told you've successfully verified your identity, i.e. the photos you've submitted all indeed belong to you, they're not ones of a

---

1This book is for Lili B. – thank you for the inspiration which eventually led to it being written.

celebrity or anything like that. But, most unexpectedly, in this one case I received a very different answer – I was told that my initial photo did not correspond to my own identity at all.

When I first read that message I was completely baffled. If I was not myself, why would I even try to verify my profile? I was obviously not pretending to be Richard Gere, Brad Pitt, George Clooney, or anyone else, famous or otherwise. I was merely presenting the app with a (supposedly) accurate representation of myself, one taken a few years before at an international conference. I was wearing a suit, my Clark Kent eyeglasses, smiling at the camera, with a modern bookshelf behind me, in what one could call a typical headshot. If memory serves me well, it was even a photo taken by a family member. I did look like myself, and I felt it accurately represented my physical identity as I would see myself in a mirror on a daily basis. Being told otherwise confused me. I really did not even know what to think about this rejection. All kinds of possibilities crossed my mind, from the extremely basic ("Is it the hair? It is kind of long and spiked right now", "Well, you *are* 8 Kg overweight", et al.), to enormously problematic ones, such as "Maybe I have some kind of strange undiagnosed mental issue which makes me see myself as very differently from what I look to others". I tried verification for a second time, and a third, and certainly a few more, hoping that I had perhaps missed a cue, or the position wasn't as faithful as it should be, or even the angle just wasn't right – and yet, the answer was always the same, as if I was indeed trying to present a photo of a celebrity as my own.

Then, at one point, still astonished over what was going on, and how strangely unexpected it all seemed to me, I decided to try something completely different. I looked up face comparison algorithms on a search engine, located a very basic one at

Faceshape.com , submitted the photo at hand, decided to compare it with another taken by myself at that same moment in time, and after some brief seconds I got a very interesting answer – the "two" people presented in the two photos were 100.00% similar. I was, at least according to this one algorithm, undoubtedly myself, and both virtual representations present in this sort of test did indeed portray me. As strange as this may sound to most readers, for a brief moment I closed my eyes and sighed in satisfaction – I now had good evidence that I was not crazy at all, the photo I was attempting to submit to this one online dating app was indeed of myself and truly represented me as I am.

But, given this initial hurdle to the usage of a simple app, I couldn't help but consider the whole problem on a much deeper philosophical level. I would have perfectly understood this whole occurrence if I was attempting to submit photos belonging to someone else. Their rejection would then be perfectly natural, and would even be most desirable, in an attempt to protect other users from the practice now called "Catfishing", which can be succinctly described as the act of presenting online photos of others as if they were our own. But, in this one case, I was in fact submitting a photo portraying me, one also belonging to me, and trying to pass along to others a virtual confirmation that such a photo was indeed my own and nobody else's. And yet, time and again this one app kept on blabbering back that I just wasn't me. I was, in a sense, now somewhat unsure of who I was at a physical level, but all the app kept on saying is that I wasn't myself, which was far from helpful in a situation where you are not intentionally faking your identity.

Hoping for some answers, or even for further clarification on what was going on, I contacted their Customer Support,

4

approached them on this whole problem, and offered to verify my account and identity in some other way – submitting a photo ID from my country, or taking a new photo of myself with a paper displaying some kind of text, tend to be absolute classics. Sadly, all I heard back from them is that the verification process always had to rely on the algorithm offered by the app, and if such resource was denying that I was myself, I naturally couldn't be myself at all. There was absolutely no flexibility in any of this, as if I was just talking to a mindless robot, not to a human being capable of adapting their speech to the circumstances at hand. Since I couldn't find any way to either confirm or deny that I was talking to a real person, I simply decided to close down my account in that one app, less than 48 hours after first registering.

This whole subject could simply end here, if it wasn't for the fact that I then decided to try out some other online dating apps and websites. Perhaps, more than searching for a relationship of any kind, I was then specially curious about the whole problem I had just faced. How could I be myself, and not be so, at the exact same point of time? Or, at the end of the day, what does it mean to be myself, and what does it ever mean to be who we are in a virtual environment?

Chapter II – The Quest for Authenticity

As someone with knowledge of Psychology at a college degree level, across the years I asked some patients to perform a task which I hoped would remind them of who they truly are, deep inside. In it, I request them to approach a mirror, look deep into their own eyes, and say or think of some words then relevant to themselves. What the content of such phrases was would depend variously from one case to the next, but all people seemed to agree that this potentially-strange process fomented a deep connection with their own inner selves. I can argue that such a thing happens because we are not used up to confronting ourselves in a such an intimate and direct way, one that may ultimately remind us that we are all human. And, through such a process, when a person looks at themselves in a mirror, unless something is terribly wrong with them at a neurological or psychological level, they can see who they are physically. So, if I was looking for my own self-identity, I felt that a similar process in my own life would undoubtedly be a great point to start at.

For this reason, as I looked at myself in a mirror, I started trying to realize who I was, from a physical standpoint. I had to wear my eyeglasses or I wouldn't be able to see anything very well – meaning, at this current point in time the usage of this accessory was not merely a cosmetic decision, but one which gave me a better quality of life. Under their lenses I could also spot my own two eyes, coloured in a dark shade of brown. I could further see that my hair was completely black, that my nose was slightly facing up, and that my ears looked a bit strange to me, in a way that I just couldn't fully put down into words yet. Later, as I would explore photos of other people, I found myself thinking about these same characteristics again –

their own noses and ears also looked strange to me, making me realize that mine were not that much different, and perhaps I was just not used up, at least at that point in time, to contemplating the way they look in such a personal and intimate way. I assume most people aren't, either.

As I followed through with this process, I realized I could jot down brief notes about specific characteristics of my face and body, ones which could partially set me apart from the rest of mankind. If, for example, my eyes are brown, and a photo presents someone with blue eyes, under normal conditions that couldn't be me at all. If I am fairly short and the person portrayed in an image looks like a giant, again it couldn't be me at all. And so on. Then, if I grabbed all possible individual characteristics and presented them in a list, through a comparison with other possibilities I would be led, step by step, to a potential representation of all my physical characteristics. Or, in a nutshell, to find my physical self-identity I would have to play a real game of "Guess Who?" with myself – brown eyes, black hair, eyeglasses, and so on, until all faces in the classic gaming board were down, ideally leaving only myself up, and so establishing that one face and body as my own. If, at the end, all the characteristics I had jotted down just weren't enough yet, I could simply introduce some more, potentially even more unique ones (such as my fingerprints), until I managed to present to others a realistic version of who I am, at a purely physical level.

Case closed? Would it be as simple as these lines may now make you believe? It could seem so, until we introduce the possibility of people who frequently look very alike, but also aren't completely the same, such as identical triplets. If one's self-identity relies solely on physical characteristics, we could potentially make the significant mistake of saying that three people looking very alike would in fact be just one and the same, which evidently isn't true. And, for that reason, if one was to find true self-identity, they would also have to contemplate more psychological elements, ones which can't be seen by the eyes but which are still there and deeply influence who we all are. Given that they cannot be proved – or disproved – as easily as physical elements, and that often only we know about certain aspects of our own internal identity, how could these ever be attained at all? If, for example, one had interviewed a young Ted Bundy in the street and had asked him if he was a serial killer, he would evidently deny it – and yet, now, many years after his death, we all know about his horrendous crimes against women. If he had never been caught, if he had never told anyone about his deeds, if nobody had ever survived his attacks, he could openly claim to be a saintly man, and likely nobody would disagree with such portrayal, specially given his immense charm. In such a case, his internal identity, and his external one, would deeply clash, resulting in a flawed portrayal of a self-identity. But how could one get around this whole problem, if at all?

I would love to present a solution to the problem in these lines, but I couldn't find one until much later. Physical self-identity was easy to judge, in a sequence of successive binary options ("does this person have the characteristic X or not?"), but initially the only way I could find to attain one's psychological identity was through self-reporting. In this sense, if I had met Ted Bundy in the middle of the street and he denied being a killer, I would just have to take his word for it. Given the indisputable truth that "people lie", as they often do when they have something to gain out of it, this may even explain why most online dating apps and websites verify physical identity but almost never a psychological one – for all we know, behind each person could be hidden a new serial killer, and yet people seem to consistently leave this problem aside, as if such a breed was utterly extinct in our day and age.

To get around this enormous problem, it seems that some people have now devised a technique they call "proof of life". Its kernel is fairly simple – talk to someone online, make up some kind of vague reason to request their Instagram page (or a similar social media), and see if the photos they present do match who they claim to be and, perhaps even more importantly, how they claim to live their lives. This could even be a very good solution to the whole problem, of course, until you realize that when people want to trick us there are endless ways to do it. If, for example, someone wants to claim they have saved Pope Francis' life, we would certainly take that unusual information with a huge grain of salt, and consider them as complete liars from the get-go, until they showed us a photo perhaps similar to this one:

2

---

2 For evident privacy reasons my own face is censored in all photos presented in this book. As you may naturally assume, none of the photos, specially the ones presented in later chapters, were originally presented in such a censored form.

Created specifically for this book, this is a photo of someone with my face giving a huge hug to Pope Francis in the Vatican Square – but *please* ignore the flying dinosaur on the left, "it was just casually passing by the whole scene at that very same moment in time". Such a strange element was included here only as a joke, since scammers do not usually present their falsity in such an evident way. And so, the whole idea of judging one's "proof of life" is a mere fantasy, and little else, that some people try to use to make themselves feel more safe, while disregarding the ultimate fact that we can know very little about someone's own psychological identity unless they want to share it with us in complete good faith.

All these things considered, one's own self-identity can so be divided into two essential parts. The first one, the physical part of our identity, can be verified in a fairly simple way, as already described above. However, the second one, the psychological part of who we are, can only be attained by those we permit to access it, either through direct self-reporting, or via indirect access (such as through our actions, e.g. "he was really rude to a waiter, he is probably a jerk to everyone else too"). And this seemed fairly simple to me. For that reason, armed with this new knowledge I decided to create a whole new online dating profile. I now knew that to be myself I'd have to present not only more than one photo, but also attempt a true representation of my internal nature. Hopefully, this would allow me to avoid the same problem I had experienced before.

Chapter III – Unforeseen Challenges

When creating this new profile, I indeed decided to attempt to make it as real as I could. Although I was (now) aware that I could give people a thousand non-physical lies and they'd probably not be able to spot any of them, I decided that if I was going to create a new profile through what I had learned, I also had to be as honest as I could – no pterosaurs over the scene, just me, myself, and I, in an approach as honest as possible. For this reason, although I was already perfectly aware of how popular some types of photos tend to be – for example, for men a photo cuddling a puppy or a kitten is always a very good choice – I did not want to rely in any such tricks. I wanted this to be *my* profile, and present me as I really am, in spite of what all other people did with theirs. And so, I felt my photos should represent different parts of my (real) personality and my (real) life. After near-endless debates with friends around what could work and what possibly wouldn't (me reading a book would be fine, me holding the Durandal in France wouldn't), I decided to select six photos. Why this number, instead of only one (perfectly capturing my personal dislike of photos), three, seven, or any other sum? Simply because the very first app I was attempting at the time suggested such a number, advising that users with it would get presented to more viewers. I could never confirm that such an information was indeed true, but at the time I decided to just take their word for it.

For the initial photo, I would present viewers with a very simple one – the same one I discussed in the first chapter, one of myself smiling at the camera, dressed in a suit, with a bookshelf behind me, since I felt this captured my face and my smile wonderfully. Then, in no particular order, you'd also see me climbing the stairs of a roman amphitheater, smiling while seemingly ignoring the camera, with the sun overlooking the scene from behind the walls of this wonderful monument, a good representation of my love for the Antiquity and Middle Ages. Next one presented me browsing the shelves of an old, second hand, bookstore, a huge smile gracing my lips, so representing my passion for old books and the literature of yore. There was also a casual photo of me having breakfast at a coffee shop (to present the idea I can also be a very down to earth person), one of myself hiking in the forest with a red book in my hand (a dual view of my passion for exploration, both physical and intellectual), and one where I was presented meditating in the garden of a local buddhist monastery (which, as odd as it may seem, was an allusion to the fact I once almost became a monk). Overall, I expected all of these to represent myself, not in an ideal way, but as realistically as I could – and, fortunately, this time around I did manage to verify my profile without any hassle, apparently confirming that the person in the photos was indeed me and nobody else.

But I also felt that, although the majority of people seem to think that online dating is all about the photos (in fact, most female profiles I read across the years were often empty, as if to say they only had their good looks, and absolutely nothing else, to give to the viewer), I also wanted to present myself, as I really am, in all the profile text. I wanted it to be a realistic representation of some limited sections of my psychological identity. Admittedly, perhaps some parts of what I decided to write were a bit over the top (e.g. "The first thing people notice about me – 'He is a bit unusual, but also the most interesting person I have ever met in my life', a quote from a friend"), but I genuinely felt they represented who I am, with my own various personal strengths and weaknesses. Neither did I consciously want to overplay the first, nor diminish the second, and so I simply went through every potential section of the profile and filled them all with my own writing the best I could. To do this, when offered a prompt such as "The thing that keeps me in shape", I would truly reflect on the whole subject for as long as it took, and tried to create an answer that not only fitted what I was being asked, but also provided some indirect evidence about who I really am inside, e.g. "I love walking everywhere. Then, I sit down, meditate for a few hours, and come back home".

A few days later I started talking to people I felt some kind of interest in. Some of them seemed more keen in talking to me than others, and I believe that is perfectly okay, something which undoubtedly occurs to everyone in places like these. I also did notice that most people seemed not to have read the profile at all, either asking questions for which the answer was already there (e.g. "why are you even single?"), or showing themselves absolutely clueless about elementary aspects of my identity (e.g. "so, how old are you?"). At times like those, I simply took a deep breath, groaned a bit, and imagined that someone better would eventually appear, which seems to be a common fantasy in this kind of places, with many other friends admitting to also have felt similar things. So, I just kept on going, trying to talk to some new people here and there, until the entire situation came crashing down in a very unexpected way...

Part II

Chapter IV – Adapting Strategies

One day, I was simply talking to someone from Madrid, in Spain, and instead of even attempting to have any kind of real conversation with me, this one person just kept on insisting that the six photos were not my own. When asked very directly about it, and in spite of the fact my profile was even verified through the app's own algorithm, this one person time and again insisted that my photos did not represent me. She never provided me any real explanation for her words, which would have been immensely helpful (and I'd definitely want to feature her answer here), but still returned endlessly to that same subject. Was she setting it all up to eventually ask for my Instagram account name, a very popular strategy among those looking to inflate their number of followers? Perhaps, but if so that part of the situation ultimately never unfolded – I soon got tired of it and decided to block her, so preventing her from further interacting with me.

In general, this one dialogue could seem like no big deal, but since some other people also seemed to approach me exclusively on the content of the photos, while completely disregarding all the content of my profile text, I decided that I had to change something significant about my approach to online dating. Since I felt people were placing just too much emphasis on my six photos – not even their content, but just the way *I* looked in them – and then seemed to care little about who I was as a person, I hoped that by removing some, and keeping what I felt was a bare minimum – just three portrayals of who I am – this would start to attract a different kind of audience, one wanting to get to know the real me, instead of approaching me solely over my (supposed) good looks.

What three photos would they be? For the sake of variety and honest self-representation I decided they had to present completely different parts of my being, instead of featuring the exact same topic or scheme again and again – too many books, for example, could lead people to imagine me as a bookworm who never leaves the house. Following through with the whole idea, I felt that two of the previously selected photos would still fit nicely in this new role, but I also needed a new headshot without the presence of books, and so I opted to take a beautiful one in the local forest. Given this simplification of my profile, those who visited it would then be confronted with just three photos, as presented below:

As you can easily see in here, there was nothing particularly amazing or off-putting about these photos, they were all

verified as my own by the app's system and essentially
supposed to represent three different but significative aspects
of my identity. First, the person who loves hiking and spending
time in the forest, in a headshot where the sun's position among
the trees gave me an aura of sorts. Second, the cultured man
who cherishes visiting monuments of the past, in the middle of
one such exploration. Third, the lover of old books, browsing a
quaint local store in search of his next literary finding. They
were not overly impressive photos, but they weren't completely
casual shots either. And, for me, that was perfectly okay,
because I was trying to portray myself as I am, not as an ideal
man who, like the sirens of yore, would try to lure people into
the rocks with his songs, a metaphor for all the very beautiful
photos which do not always accurately represent the profile
creator. And the idea worked as intended, perhaps even better
than I had expected. For a few days I was able to talk to people
who actually seemed interested in getting to know me as I
really am.

But then, one day I woke up in the morning and noticed that
the first of these three photos was completely gone from
OkCupid, one of the apps and websites I was trying at the time.
I knew I evidently had not removed it myself, and nobody else
could have accessed my account either. I could not understand
what was going on at all, because I just couldn't see this one
photo having anything wrong about it. It was just a headshot
taken in the forest, and nothing else. I found this specially
strange because, according to their own rules and internal
information, they tend to send people an e-mail warning when
they remove any photos, but I myself had never received one,
either at that point in time or even later. Very confused about
the whole thing, but also believing that the person from Madrid
had perhaps maliciously reported me, and subsequently some
new member of the site's staff could have accidentally removed

it, I put the missing photo back in its place and wrote a short message to their Customer Support, trying to get an explanation about what had happened. And then, I waited for an answer.

Chapter V – Customer Support Conundrum and Identity Verification

At this point I would love to tell you that I soon talked to their staff, who were all clearly understanding human beings and always very sympathetic to me, and everything was then quickly sorted out, but that was not what happened, at all. If it had been so, perhaps this book would never have been written at all. Instead, the very next day I yet again woke up in the morning and their staff had removed *all three* of my photos. I just did not even know what to think about this. But then, some limited hope rose – one "Yolygen Alayon" replied to my message to their Customer Support with the following words, which deserve to be quoted here in their complete form:

Thanks for reaching out to OkCupid! I understand you wish to re-upload your photos. Let me assist you further with this.

[My name here], *In today's world, we must be conscious of the photos we post online. With that in mind, we show that you uploaded an inappropriate photo. This photo does not meet the OkCupid photo guidelines.*

We value you as a member of our community, however, if this continues, we'll be forced to close your account. Your success is important to us and we wouldn't want this to impact your ability to find your perfect match.

While we do not make specific content recommendations, your photos must follow these guidelines:

- No nudity or sheer/see-through clothing
- No drawings, caricatures, or other illustrations

- No copyrighted images
- No identifying information (ie: license plates, email or web addresses, visible street address numbers, etc.)
- No illegal acts or violence
- No minors only (without an adult included in the photo)
- No rotated photos; they must be facing upright
- No specific military identification
- No shirtless photos out of context (i.e., indoors, not at beach pool or exercising) or shirtless mirror selfies

Also, keep in mind the following:

- You must appear in the primary photo.
- Your photo cannot contain any information that could potentially identify who you are (company badge, license plate, etc)
- Image files must be received in an approved format (jpeg, bmp, gif, tiff, wmf, ico, emf, or exif) and should be larger than 100k and less than 5 MB.
- The ideal pixel dimensions should be at least 300 x 400. (To determine pixel dimensions and image format, right-click on your photo and view the properties of the image.)

For reference, our Terms of Use can be referenced at the following link: [link here]

Let us know if we can be of additional help.

Far from being helpful, this one message only contributed to confuse me even further. Supposedly, I had posted one photo – notice the usage of the singular, "an inappropriate photo" – that did not meet their guidelines, and so they were forced to remove it. In its essence this could certainly make some sense, but if it was so, why had they now removed *all* my three photos? I just did not understand what was going on, at all. Hoping to find an answer to the problem, I carefully went through all their guidelines and rules one by one – there was no nudity; no drawings or illustrations; no copyrighted images; no identifying information; nothing either illegal or violent; no minors; no rotated photos; nothing related to the military; no shirtless photos; and I did appear in all of my photos (or so I thought, as you will understand later). So, simply put, this one staff member told me that one of my photos had violated their rules, subsequently removed all three of them, couldn't tell me what was wrong with any, and even provided me with a set of rules which wasn't even helpful in any way. Or, if you prefer to see it in a potentially more realistic way, chances are that they incompetently sent me a copy-pasted message and hoped that would solve the whole situation. But it just didn't.

After much thinking, I assumed that the only possibility was that they, for some kind of really strange reason, supposed it was not me in any of the photos I had submitted, in spite of the evident fact I had previously verified my account, an act which should have ensured that all the submitted content was indeed my own. And, to me, this also seemed like an extremely dangerous point – if I had indeed verified my profile as my own, and if people saw the verification sign in my profile (as they did), but at the end of the day I was (supposedly) not portraying myself at all, this could naturally mean that other people, ones attempting to perform the most various misdeeds, could have their own profiles falsely verified. If this was indeed true, it could also mean that whenever you see a verified profile in an online dating app, this does not ensure that the person behind it is ever who they claim to be, in spite of the fact the app and website constantly claiming otherwise, i.e. "verify your profile and others will know you're really you".

And so, I felt I had to prove to their Customer Support that I was indeed myself, and if I failed to do so it could ultimately mean that the verification algorithms for online dating apps are extremely flawed, which would even explain the previous rejection of one of my photos in another app. I decided to do exactly that, still hoping that all that was going on was just a very honest mistake on their side, and absolutely nothing more.

But how would I ever be able to prove I was indeed myself in the three photos I've shown you before, and nobody else was represented there? I decided to try to present to them what I felt was a foolproof case. First, and for undoubtedly the most important point of them all, I stated that I had previously gone through their photo verification process and successfully passed it, even presenting some evidence of this. Along with it, I also sent them a photo of my country's ID with Yolygen's name written in a paper sheet under it, and I also took a candid selfie with the same legal document visibly held in one of my hands. If this still wasn't enough, I even sent them a screenshot of the result of a face comparison algorithm, showing that the first photo in my profile matched my ID's by an impressive 100.00%, and also matched my own new selfie by the exact same 100.00%. All these things considered, either I was indeed myself, and the photos were truly my own, or something terribly wrong was going on with their computer systems or human personnel.

This message was sent to them on the 22nd of March 2024. Having received no answers in the following weeks, in spite of some insistence once a week, I then decided to contact their legal department, hoping for an extra-judicial resolution to the problem (as suggested by their website's legal print), but I also did not receive any answers from them either. This was all extremely frustrating, but such lack of interest in actually helping their users seems to be a common constant in support personnel from online dating apps and websites. Finally, I tried to request all my data under the GDPR, as it is my right as a citizen of Europe. I hoped this additional development would not only force them to break their silence, but also allow me to retrieve my previously-removed photos. Obtaining them through their own services would make it possible for me to easily show that the one person portrayed in all my previously submitted photos was always one and the same – only me and nobody else! And so, on the 19th of April 2024 I finally got an answer back from someone who simply identified herself as "Kimi":

We have received your recent data request. For your protection and the protection of all of our users, we cannot release any personal data without first obtaining proof of identity. Before we are able to provide you with your data we will need to verify your identity and ownership of the account.

To help us verify your identity, please send us a redacted copy of your Government ID (e.g. passport or driver's license), showing only your name, photo, and date of birth. We'll use your ID for verification purposes only and then promptly delete it. Emailing us a copy of your ID will result in the fastest response time. If you prefer, however, you may instead send us a redacted copy of your ID by postal mail to the address listed in the "How to Contact Us" section of our Privacy Policy. Again, we'll use your ID for verification purposes only and then promptly destroy it. We may require further verification of your identity, for example, if the materials you provide do not establish your identity to a sufficient degree of certainty.

We will proceed with your request if we are able to successfully verify your identity. If you previously closed your account, please note that your personal data may be unavailable because it may have been deleted in accordance with our Privacy Policy. If data is available, there is some information we cannot release to you, including information that would likely reveal personal information about other users. This notably includes messages you receive on OkCupid, which are not provided to protect the privacy of the senders.

OkCupid Privacy Team

This message, the only real reply about the whole subject I got after almost a month, was all about the GDPR, but it also completely ignored the problem I was having with my three photos. It was as if they had decided they just couldn't care any less about what they had done, in a robotic copy-paste response extremely common in the Customer Support teams for online dating apps and websites. And so, I further insisted on wanting to know what was really going on, and the next day I quickly received another e-mail from "Kimi" (only the relevant information is now quoted here):

As for your photos being removed from our system AI photos are not allowed on our platform. You will need to post photos of you that are not AI or artificial in any way.

Yet again, I was completely baffled by this new answer. It even seemed just too absurd to be true. If "Yolygen" had previously accused me of not meeting some undisclosed point of their photo guidelines, this new member of their Customer Support was now changing that original explanation and accusing me of a completely different thing, of having submitted AI-generated photos to their system. This was particularly strange because, at that point in time, they did not even have any rules forbidding people from doing so (and yes, I checked for it), and when I pointed this out to "Kimi", she subsequently gave me an even more astonishing answer:

Per our Community Guidelines:
"While our Community Guidelines cover most instances of moderator action, it is not an exhaustive list, and we do retain the right to ban anyone from OkCupid if we believe you have violated the Community Guidelines, Terms of Use, misused our Services, or behaved in a way that OkCupid regards as inappropriate or unlawful, on or off our Services."

Generally known in the IT industry as the "Moderator Discretion" rule, this threat basically says their company has the right to ban – not remove the photos, as they had done to me, but completely ban from their platform – anyone they want, for any reason they want, at any time they want, even if the person has done absolutely nothing wrong. So, if, for example, one was to confront a member of their Customer Support staff with the fact that when a user first registers their number of likes is quickly inflated through the usage of bots placed in Kenya and the Philippines (which would generally be very low-interest countries for the bulk of western users), and that this is done in the hopes of getting potentially desperate new users to sign up for premium accounts (which would allow them to see who had "liked" their profile), said person could be banned for knowing about this evidently illegal practice from the company – one, in fact, that their parent group was even already sued for in the past!

And although the whole idea may be considered fair enough – their house, their rules, one could say – the implication behind

"Kimi"'s words was, in my view, just too problematic to ignore – if my photos were indeed being seen by their staff as "AI-generated", that would mean that false photos were able to bypass their verification algorithms and be considered as truthful representations of a user. This would also mean that any scammer savvy enough about the subject could create some false photos, submit them to this app or website, falsely verify their account, and pretending to be someone they are not, scam as many people as they want – and this, while the person being scammed would be left crying and saying "oh, oh, but their profile was verified, I thought they were real!!"

Perhaps even more worrying, if such a person was ever to face a problem like this one, and then decided to contact the company over what had happened to them, *OkCupid* could then simply ban them under the aforementioned "Moderator Discretion" rule, to try to hide away the whole case. And this whole potential situation still gets even worse – since they never have to provide their reasons for banning someone, stating that they just cannot do this "for privacy reasons", this one person, first scammed by one of the company's users and then further maliciously removed by the intermediary party, would never even know what had really happened to them. Most people would not have the time or the resources to take the whole company to court over any of this.

Chapter VI – Algorithmic Insights

Following from the essential implication established in the previous chapter, either my photos were indeed my own – and also not "AI-generated" at all – or it would be possible to create such fake photos and subsequently use them to verify a profile. But would this truly be possible, or was it all merely an unfounded theory? Out of sheer scientific curiosity, I decided to test this possibility.

To begin the whole process, I needed access to at least one photo that could never be considered as AI-generated at all, and I decided I could use the one present on my national ID for this, since it would be completely impossible to deny that such a photo was indeed my own. Then, I needed some photos to compare with it, and I decided to use at least some of the six I had originally submitted to *OkCupid*. Also, I needed two entirely new photos for comparison – and so, I used a new one of me meditating, which had been taken a few days before, and also one taken in that exact same moment in time. And finally, to test if the algorithms being used were accurate, I needed to establish a control group with photos which undoubtedly were not my own and could not be considered as AI-generated either – with a satirical intent, and specially given his personal philosophies, I picked two of Ted Kaczynski, a beardless one taken in 1968 and a bearded one taken at his arrest in 1996, in both cases way before the generation of images by a computer was ever even possible. Then, I looked up four different face comparison algorithms, and went on to test if I was the person in my photos or not, generating the first table you can see at the end of this book.

Interpreting its results, the probability of my face being present in the relevant photos was between 72% and 100%[3], depending on the evaluating algorithm, with this value even rising to over 84% in a comparison established with one of the two photos I had taken recently. And so, there was a very strong probability that the person portrayed in my ID, and the ones presented in the three photos at one point submitted to *OkCupid*, were indeed one and the same. This is further evidenced through the control group – my potential presence in the photos of Ted Kaczynski is never over 7%, because I was undeniably not the person represented there at all. So, all this considered, there was no indisputable reason to argue that the photos were not my own. But, regardless of what I could say about it – I was certainly a biased party in all of this problem – could they have been potentially generated by an AI? I located four algorithms to test this, and quickly created one more table with the tested data, the second you can see at the end of this book.

These other results are certainly more controversial than the previous ones, because although the photo from my ID was clearly not an AI-generated one (such probability was always under 6%), for all the remaining ones the probability of them having been created in such a way ranged between 3% and 98%, which could mean almost anything between "very unlikely" and "almost certain". Then, when compared with the control group, composed of the photos of Ted Kaczynski both with and without beard, a problem suddenly became very apparent – an original photo taken in the distant year of 1968 evidently cannot have been generated by a computer, but one of the algorithms even considered such generation as a certainty. Since a different one clearly denies that same possibility, it could indicate that the fourth algorithm was the

---

3 You may notice a "0%" result for the fourth test of the third photo. I was unable to figure out where this value came from, and ultimately decided to discard it as a potential bug in their system.

most reliable one, and following from it, it would also be possible to consider that the three "offending" photos were indeed AI generated... and so, through this data, the company would have more than enough evidence to argue that three photos could all be AI-generated, no matter how long I tried to dispute it.

Although I am ultimately unable to explain why any of these algorithms were "recognizing" my photos in such a way – barring the fact that they make mistakes, like in the case of the "Photo Taken Right Now" (which had, in fact, been taken in that very moment), or Ted's photos – I felt they could be incorrectly seeing red flags where there were really none. How else could even be explained that a photo taken in that very same moment had an 82% chance of having been generated by AI? It evidently seemed very odd, but unfortunately, and unlike I had expected at the very beginning, resorting to this scientific data could be used to claim that my three photos were indeed AI-generated, and no matter how many times I denied it, that wouldn't change the conclusions derived from any of the data I had collected.

Soon after, I finally received the results of my GDPR request. In them, I noticed that all the past photos were not presented there at all – instead, their common status was generally shown in the report with the following pieces of information:

Status: User Picture Inactive
Caption: [none was present here, because I hadn't used any captions for my photos]
Uploaded: [date and time here]
Selfie Verified (Y/N): Y
Selfie Verified Timestamp: [a number with 13 digits was presented here]

Although this could indicate their company truly deletes submitted photos when you remove them from your profile, as their Privacy Policy requires, it should be noted that in a previous e-mail "Kimi" had still seemingly seen my removed photos and even considered them as AI-generated. Either she was completely lying to me, or in spite of the fact they claim to be deleting removed photos, they actually weren't. I couldn't find any real ways to test this. What was indisputable, however, is that at least one of said removed photos was "selfie verified", and so, according to their own claims, that one photo was mine and accurately portrayed myself – and yet, they removed it from my profile without any consent from me, first under some very vague reference to some undisclosed rule, but later amending such false claim to instead declare that my photos, literally all of them, had all been generated by AI!

So, I presented all this evidence to them… and never got any answers about any of it, as of the date of writing of these lines. Just a few hours later I deleted the profile at hand, but an enormous question now presented itself in my mind – if one was admittedly to generate false photos through AI, as this one person claimed I had done, would such a strategy be able to bypass the verification algorithms of dating apps?

Part III

Chapter VII – Ethical Dilemmas

In order to test this aggravating point, I knew I had to throw all ethics out of the window for the opportunity to study something which, in my view, could be extremely dangerous for all the users of dating apps. Would I be able to pretend being someone else with the help of AI, and in spite of such falseness still get my account verified? And also, generating an absurdly false photo, would the same dating app algorithms still allow me to verify my profile with it?

For the first part, I obtained three photos from a random instagrammer and tried to verify my account using them – naturally, the whole process failed. Then, I tried the exact same thing by actually generating, through an AI algorithm, a photo of a person in a boat accompanied by a supposed representation of the Loch Ness Monster – once again, and as it could also be predicted well in advance, this second photo did not pass any of the verification algorithms either.

So far so good, the whole verification algorithm seemed to be working as intended and protecting the users of dating apps and websites, but this rejection was evidently happening because neither the face nor the body present in the photos was mine at all. If I wanted to truly test this potential problem, I knew I had to take it all one step further. So, I then resorted to an online "face swap" algorithm, adding my own face to all the photos obtained in the previous steps, and even going through an additional step of flipping them and significantly changing their saturation so they wouldn't show up in image recognition systems like *TinEye*. This time around, all the photos I submitted were easily verified as my own, showing that one attempting to do all kinds of misdeeds in online dating apps could easily do so by means of "face swap" algorithms, which basically just superimpose a whole new face into previously existing photos.

This was a troubling finding, but was it a one-time problem, perhaps exclusive to one or two of the apps I was trying it on, or a more generalized situation? To test this, I took all the same photos to as many different dating apps as I could find, going as far as presenting them all in a single profile at the same time, and the results ended up astonishing me, because I truly hoped that at least some of them would have noticed the very different body types or hair colors, among other potential elements, presented in those various representations.

But they never did. Instead, for the first scenario, with the photos of an instagrammer with my own face added to them, every single one of the apps I tested allowed me to verify the submitted content as being truthfully my own. So, if I wanted to pretend to be a very tall and super-muscly guy (something which always seems quite popular with the ladies), I would have absolutely no trouble doing so. For the second one, an image purely generated by AI with a notoriously false element present in it, only two apps rejected it – through their Customer Support staff, the first later openly admitted that they do a manual verification of all submitted photos and this one was "clearly fake" (their exact words), while the second's staff warned me that I could only keep such a strange photo in my profile if I also submitted at least one of myself that was clearly not edited or AI-generated at all.

The admission that at least one dating app does an initial and manual verification of all submitted photos particularly impressed me. They were not a huge one, like *Tinder*, and if a small and fairly new app was managing to do this, one can certainly suppose that much bigger ones, with their more impressive resources, could also do so – and yet, they don't seem to do so at all, or they would have caught the evidently-false "Loch Ness Monster" photo in their net and rejected it. But why don't they do this? The answer has to be a very blunt one – this would take a lot of extra resources and cost additional money, and they just don't care enough about the safety of any of their users to protect them from scammers, murderers, or even worse people.

These results were, in my personal opinion, both extremely problematic and intriguingly tantalizing. At first, this may mean that absolutely anyone you see with a "verified" profile in online dating apps and websites may not even be who they claim to be, in spite of the fact said services (falsely) assuring us that their algorithm always ensures so. But, at same time, if we consider that online dating is almost exclusively about the photos, this opens the possibility that people may now start creating and displaying truly unique images, ones that were previously impossible in "normal" photos, but that can now portray people in ways that we never considered possible before. If we could take away, once and for all, the idea of judging online photos exclusively on the person's attractiveness, and instead start judging them as an expression of a person's deepest kernel and originality, we would be able to gain a much better access to who they are deep inside, via the many ways in which they choose to express themselves to others.

At this point in time, maybe that could have been the lesson to take from all this book. Although verification algorithms in online dating apps are absolutely more unreliable and flawed than we're constantly led to believe, promising a fake safety which cannot even be trusted at all, there is often an intriguing human element in the profiles we come across. If we could learn to enjoy their uniqueness, we could also be able to find out more about people's internal self-identity than we ever judged possible. Consider, for example, the "Loch Ness Monster" photo from above – we can either reject this one person for putting in front of us such a clearly-fake photo, or we can see such an image as a very innovative expression of who they are deep inside, and then be very intrigued about why would they even choose to represent themselves like that.

Reflecting on the whole dissertation presented in this small book until now, when my initial photo was rejected by a dating app algorithm, perhaps the right question to ask was not about my own self-identity, or why the content itself was being put aside by a non-human entity, but one regarding why people feel the necessity to rely so much on such "verification" algorithms, as if a mere circle present on a dating profile was an absolutely undeniable piece of evidence that the person on the other side of the screen is always who they claim to be, both physically and psychologically. Instead of such a lofty promise, the result of that algorithm only attests that a similar face – just a face, and not even a full body – may potentially be present in the person behind that profile, and that says very little about who they are.

In fact, can you still remember how physically attractive and charming Ted Bundy used to be? Relying on this "verified" icon from a dating app, a woman could, and most likely would, have been charmed into going out with him, and she would potentially end up being murdered, as many were back in the day... and who wouldn't want to avoid such a definite fate in their lives? The only real way to do so is not via a physical self-identity, the only aspect that these algorithms can ever test, but through the judgment of one's psychological identity over time. My hope, at the end of this chapter, which was originally thought as the book's final, was for a collective awakening to this significant truth. A truth urging us to look beyond the algorithmic facade and embrace the richness of a more genuine human connection, which can only occur if we learn that we're talking to actual living human beings, and not merely pretty pictures adorning a screen.

Chapter VIII – Identity and Perception in Digital Dating

A few days after writing the previous chapter I realized that I still needed a few more steps to conclude the circle started by the initial chapter. I still needed to present what all of this taught me not only about Online Dating in itself, but also about self-identification in the digital age.

Through the various experiments presented in the previous chapters, I learned a person is generally considered as "real", and worthy of credit by others, in dating apps and websites if their submitted photos, and a new one taken in controlled conditions, match in the essential points of their face. Such a process does not even consider one's body, or the overall content of the photos the person presents, but simply part of the content of their face, as if people only lied about their facial good looks, which is completely absurd. The whole idea also completely forgets to take into consideration the psychological aspects that make a person who they are. In such a context, a very attractive serial killer could perhaps be more desirable than a good man with average looks. And this idea, if correct, would be extremely problematic, since dating a dangerous criminal does not tend to be a very good idea. But how could I test it?

As you may recall, I had previously created a profile which represented me fairly well at a psychological level, and I even presented in this book the three photos I eventually selected for it. I was very happy with both its text and its photos, and when I took it all to an AI-evaluation algorithm, it not only called my profile "very unique", but even rated its content between an 8 and a 9 out of 10, something which seemed very good to me. Unfortunately, not only did such a profile get a very limited number of likes on a weekly basis, but the kind of people I truly wanted to get to know better would very infrequently, if at all, even connect with it. This problem remained even in situations where I was allowed to send them an initial message, one where I always stated why I wanted to get to know them better. I was puzzled over the whole thing, because I assumed that if people shared some interests, or some crucial elements of their personality, they could like to meet someone else like them – and yet, they didn't seem to. So, I was led to think that there was clearly something in the self-representation of that profile which didn't appeal to other people. But what could the problem be? The content of the text, the photos, or something more unexpected? I wanted to know, so I could improve my profile, if nothing else.

So, as an initial step, I decided to retain all the three photos but also completely remove all the text present in that recreated profile. If I was saying something specially wrong, or perhaps very off-putting, in it, this removal would possibly have led to a higher number of likes. However, the low number of likes kept persisting, allowing me to theorize that the problem was not in the text at all. And so, I decided to delete this profile.

Then, I created an entirely new one and gave it almost precisely the same text as before, writing just a single new sentence among its written content – "This is a fake profile, created to test something". For its photos, I then used not ones of myself, or even ones I felt represented my identity well, but three pictures generated by an AI algorithm, which mimed the kind most men successful in dating apps usually submit. The selected images can be seen below:

Simply put, these were a selfie showing the face very well, a full-body shot, and a pseudo-contemplative photo. A lot could be written here about each of these, but even with the absence of my (now-censored) face in the pictures above, you may be able to spot they look like photos of two or three completely different people. I can explain that such differences were completely intended, because if I was going to use AI-generated photos, I wanted to make it all as absurdly obvious as possible. The notorious phrase alluding to this as a "fake profile" would indicate such false identity even further.

However, in spite of their differing visual content and that enormous red flag in the text, just because I had "face swapped" my own visage into these photos, that allowed me to verify this profile as a completely truthful one. And, soon after, if the previous – and very realistic – profile had experienced less than seven likes per week, this new one received over 100 in the first 24 hours[4]. Then, when I tried to talk to those people, I invariably ended up noticing they hadn't even read anything

---

4 A more precise number is impossible to present in these lines, since the counter in the various apps and websites seemed to cap at that number. Whether the people liking this profile, and the next ones, were just 101 or over a million will have to remain unknown.

in my profiles at all, regardless of the app I was trying this whole thing in. People just cared about the photos, they didn't care about the text at all, and it seemed that just because the profile was "verified", they trusted that all the photos were of myself, despite the fact my hair, face and body looked significantly different in each of them.

Was it all about the pretty photos? Did people just want those, regardless of who was behind the actual profile, as already theorized? Their obsession with said images, to the point they repeatedly ignored what should have been very evident red flags, started to make me feel physically sick. I wanted to puke, but I also felt I still needed to know the answer. I needed to find out what would happen if people had to pick between two profiles sharing the same text but differing in a single photo – a simply pretty one which said very little about me, versus one which truly captured my uniqueness. I could worry about the real-world implications later, for now I only wanted to test this.

So, I created two new profiles. For the first I tried to recreate one of the AI-generated photos as faithfully as I could, using only my own body, my clothes, and the local houses from where I live. For the second I took a truly unique photo of me in a type of monk garb, with a rosary in a meditative pose, a representation alluding both to my passion for meditation and the fact I had almost become a monk in the past. As you can easily understand, the former was a purely generic image, while the latter truly represented the kind of person I am. Since both profiles shared every single word of text, people judging them would have to rely on the only photo contained in each of them. And what happened? Simply put, few people liked the second one over a week, while the first had already reached the cap of 100 likes in a single day. I deleted both profiles, but this made me feel uncomfortable, given its potential implications. I now knew that if I was to explore the problem of self-identity in the digital age, I still needed one last step.

Chapter IX – The Illusion of Authenticity in Online Dating

Going back to the initial chapters, this whole exploration had began out of an exploration of my own self-identity. Although I now knew who I am, I also realized that people in online dating apps and websites only seemed to care about photos, completely forgetting there was actually a real human being behind them. So, a huge question rose in my head – between myself, in all that it means to be me; and a completely idealistic version of who I am, built on the previous findings of this book's chapters; who would people want?

I decided to start by creating a profile which captured very accurately the person I am. The first photo was a headshot of me in Osaka (Japan), smiling a lot, with many beautiful blossoming cherry trees and a traditional bridge placed behind me, a slight blur effect in the background further emphasizing my face. The second was the same meditation photo from the previous chapter, obviously not censored. The third presented a compilation of four of my adventures in the shape of stained glass – although a very unorthodox image, I felt this would further capture my love for art and my adventurous spirit. The fourth was a completely candid photo of me reading in a coffee shop, with people even being able to read the unusual book's title. The fifth was one of me resting in the forest, during the so-called "golden hour", smiling at the camera while in an amazing landscape. The final one, where such a possibility was available, was a video of me petting some wild horsies in their natural environment, a piece of content everyone I showed it to said was absolutely perfect for a profile and really captured my natural sweetness.

I felt each single one of these photos captured very well who I am, but I also enriched the profile content with extensive written information about myself. Each section was never too long, ranging between one and three phrases. For example, the bio read "I am someone deeply passionate about Art, Humanities, Music, Mysticism, Social Sciences, quaint hikes, forgotten places, saving the world, and finding humor in life. I prefer real connections instead of Social Media and Photos (of people). I know I'm not everyone's cup of tea, but if you're tired of the usual and instead want to meet someone truly unique, send me a message." As further examples, to the prompt "I like to make...", I answered "People smile. Whether I know them intimately or not, there's always something magical in turning one's frowny face upside down."; and to the prompt "This item makes me feel at home...", I answered "An old rosary, its beads now worn smooth by years of use, reminds me of the tranquillity I once found in prayer and reflection in the forest." Clearly, this would not be a run-of-the-mill profile, but that of a truly intriguing person – and, yet again, I felt each single word of the bio and answers perfectly captured the person I am.

Then, I had to create a profile with an idealistic version of who I am. The first photo was to have me holding a puppy. The second was a selfie in what seemed to be a work table. The third was me just standing in front of a house, well dressed and smiling. The fourth had me with a coat looking at the sea. Yes, you may even be able to recognise these as the re-enacted versions of the photos mentioned in the previous chapter, plus the addition of one with a supposed pet. Again, be sure to notice these photos said little, if anything even significative, about who I am.

What about the text for this second profile? The bio simply read "Passionate about many things", while the only prompt I included, "True or false?" was answered in the following way

"The dog is not mine, it's only here to get me more likes."
Once more, through this textual information you would get to
know almost nothing about myself, excluding the fact I could
literally be using a puppy just to get more "likes".

Soon after, I took both profiles for the proverbial spin. The first
got barely any "likes" – over a week it hadn't even reached 20
– while the second got over 100 in a single day. So far so good,
this was all fairly predictable by now, but something more
troubling suddenly started happening – when the first profile
did match with someone, more often than not the person
showed little, if any, real interest in talking to me – and can you
imagine being unmatched because, on your fifth message to a
person who claims to love travels, you ask her if she enjoys
visiting monuments too? For the second profile, however, long
conversations often ensued... and I was never really
"unmatched", even when I tried to show as little interest in the
person as possible, either by repeatedly replying with one-word
answers, or by quickly pulling sexual topics on them just to try
to push their buttons.

Although this somewhat mimed the findings of another
research I had conducted in the past, and which I have
presented in a previous book of this series, it was still upsetting
and completely stunning. I had assumed that, between generic
photos and truly unique ones, people would prefer the second,
but experience proved otherwise. I had assumed that people
would like well-written profiles, but experience proved
otherwise. And, perhaps more problematic than these two, I
had assumed that people would like to have real conversations,
but not only did they dislike them from the first profile, but
were also perfectly okay with horrible conversations from the
second. I did not even know what to think about all this, since
it made it seem that although people consistently claim to want

the first kind of profile, in reality they clearly seem to prefer the second.

The kernel of my identity, the way I chose to portray the psychological aspect of my being in an online dating app or website, either through unique photos or text, did not seem to matter at all. My individuality mattered little, only pretty pictures did. I now knew who I was, but it seemed that if I wanted to have any kind of real success in dating apps and websites, I would have to deny my identity and, instead, present others with a kind of beautiful normality they repeatedly saw in others. All my many achievements in life meant nothing at all – a single pretty picture in a predictable position appeared to be more desirable than anything I had ever accomplished, an idea even repeatedly exacerbated by the fact people weren't even reading my profile's textual content at all, since they never commented on any of it, even when the content at hand would naturally have elicited interest.

And so, the lesson to be learned from online dating apps and websites, at the level of both physical and psychological self-identification, indeed appears to be a very basic one – forget who you really are, nobody cares about that. Your accomplishments in life mean nothing. Your uniqueness means nothing. All that people care about is predictable physical beauty in a verified photo, and only if said photos are considered as satisfying enough will they then care to try to learn about who you are, even if at a very superficial level.

At the very end, that is how I came up with the title for this small book. The whole idea of *Join Online Dating, Get Raped!* may seem shocking, but that is precisely what people seem to be risking way too much nowadays – in fact, out of the people I met in my studies and training in Psychology at a college level, those (fortunately few) who had been raped by someone they met online often reported this had happened on the very first date, one in which a woman had imprudently accepted going to the man's house because "he seemed like a good person" (their words)[5]. Once he locked his entrance door, he turned out being very different, and after the whole thing unfolded victims felt specially humiliated for having been so trustworthy of someone who, all things considered, they knew nothing real about, having repeatedly discarded the multiple red flags they had, in fact and repeatedly, spotted in the past. For this reason, and for the fear of being criticized by others, more often than not they didn't even want to report to the police what had happened to them.

Sadly, things like these happen because people often over-rely on app verification when such a process is, as already proved before, extremely flawed. Then, so assuming that one's photos are real and truly represent who they are, they judge people mainly based on them, forgetting that people also have an important psychological component. And, finally, they seem to find themselves extremely surprised, on a negative sense, when they expected to find a beautiful Prince Charming and, instead, ended up with a kind of new Ted Bundy, one who didn't really care about who they are, just as they hadn't cared to properly get to know the person either. It is, in a sense, as a blind person leading another through the streets, each attempting to share the fewest significant things about themselves, while also fantasizing the most about the wholly static images in front of them.

---

5 I never found such a case with a man, likely because sexual abuse against men is widely known to be under-reported.

The same idea was further confirmed by some of the people I discussed this whole problem with. They provided completely robotic and horizontal explanations for all of it, ones where *they* were never to blame for any of it, *the other person* always was, because in spite of seeming like something very positive online (where they were, as already understood above, judged exclusively on the photo content), when met in person the psychological identity of those other people was very different from originally supposed. And this may seem like a strange thing, until you realize that people are being forced to fake the kernel of their identity to get more "likes" and, subsequently, dates.

And I know what you may be thinking on all of this, because people always told me that exact same thing – "Be yourself, that'll lead to fewer but better matches, ones from people who want to get to know the real you. Those people will like you just the way you are." But, at the end of the day, that's a pure fantasy and nothing more – people don't seem to want uniqueness, and they hardly ever read profile content. And so, instead of being true, the aforementioned piece of conventional wisdom is an online dating app's and website's biggest internal wish, in the sense it urges people to just sit back and keep their profile open across a longer period of time, in the not-so-secret hope that one very vague day in the future someone may connect with it – and then, specially frustrated by the lack of "likes" originated by their attempt at uniqueness, they'll be more likely to purchase paid packages, only to find out that they had either previously rejected those people who "liked" them, or such revealed group is mostly composed by bots located in some far-away location. And, meanwhile, by "being yourself", the person will be completely wasting their time in a huge sea of idealistic profiles, where everyone is looking for a pretty sardine and, by "being yourself", you'll essentially be that one lonely unique tuna nobody cares about.

Perhaps that is indeed the final lesson one can learn from this book and its lines. If someone's complete identity is composed of both physical and psychological elements, and you judge them exclusively based on the first ones at a very limited level, while too often also assuming that the second will always later be of your liking, you risk being raped – either in a very real way, or on a purely metaphorical level – as part of an absurd fantasy you have created in your head.

In my own case, if I hadn't tried to verify my photo in the initial chapter, people would too often pester me about doing so, if they even talked to me at all. After I did went through that process, and tried to represent myself as unique a person as I truly am, few people still talked to me. But when I later gave them idealistic and predictable versions of my physical identity, suddenly their interest in my profile became much higher – but, at the same time, I became somewhat of a statue of a greek god, one very pretty and which could do no wrong. I had, in fact, to put myself aside, in almost all that it meant to be me (minus my face), in order to achieve any kind of success in the many platforms people use for online dating. And, at the same time, on the other side of the screen were people more than eager to consume such an ideal version of me, and just that one, when they had previously rejected the real me, in its completely unique representation.

So, let me ask you three questions, ones very fit for contemplation. When seeing a profile on online dating apps and websites, do you prefer:

- One with unique personal photos, which actually reveal a lot about the person; OR one with the typical photos everyone else uses?

- One well-written and with lots of information about the person; OR one with close to nothing written in it?

- One capable of an interesting dialogue; OR one that always shows little interest in who you are and quickly advances to sexual topics?

When asked about them, people repeatedly seem to answer positively to the first part of these questions, but this real-world experience appears to reveal that, in fact, they prefer the second. And then, they end up crying when the person they had in front of them seemed something but later proved to be a very different one... who knew?! Perhaps they would have, if they had listened more, if they had truly learned about the person in front of them, instead of just considering their surface and idealizing everything else. Who knew it could be that simple?

Epilogue

I wrote the previous chapters of this book and then decided to put the whole subject aside for some time. All was well, until one day I decided to create my own profile, not for research purposes, as one could suppose by now, but just to talk to new people. Soon after, I was confronted with the typical photo-submission step, and it hit me incredibly hard. I even developed what could be considered as symptoms of a panic attack, to the point I just could not decide what photos to present to others any more. The text-writing part was a fairly simple one, I knew who I am and it wasn't too hard to attempt to describe myself. However, when it came down to the photos, I nauseously found myself struggling with the whole thing. Would I decide to portray myself as I am, with all my own uniqueness, or give others what they want with boringly predictable photos? I just could not decide, because this simple choice was, as previously shown, a huge choice between getting many likes – one of the fake profiles had just gathered 10 more likes in less than 12 hours – and hardly anyone ever talking to me.

I went to bed and lied there, my head in a pillow, during a completely silent night, considering all the implications. Time and again, I just could not decide anything about this, at all, as a whirlwind of emotions rushed through my head. But eventually, and perhaps inspired by Aristotle's idea of "virtue lies in the middle", I decided that I could try to create a profile joining together the two elements. It'd include a photo with a borrowed pet, a really cute puppy (and which was revealed as a borrowed furry friend in the caption), among other such content. And I did try it for a few days, but it just didn't feel like myself, and also lead me to fear that cat lovers could dislike the profile, simply being misled by the potential idea I could have a pet puppy in my life.

What could I do? I had to think extensively about this for a few days, until I noticed that nothing forced me to created just one profile across apps and websites. Instead, I decided to create one more like myself in places like *OkCupid*, where there is plenty of space for written content (which I still secretly hoped some people would actually read...); and more of an idealistic version in places like *Tinder*, where images are all that matters. The first kept on getting very few likes, while the second, even after a few weeks, still gathered at least 10 each day. Soon enough, and inspired by that old accusation of having AI-generated content in my profile, I decided to create something truly unique.

This is a photo of me with a cute puppy and a kitten, which could be a completely real one. However, in order to make it more unreal, I gave the whole scene a black-and-white background, blurred the pets a bit, and added comic thought bubbles to both of them – on the left, the puppy was thinking "Plot twist: We're both CGI...", while on the right the kitten added "but [my name here]'s real, and here to make you smile!" It was supposed to be both funny and satirize typical online dating photos, crowded with idealistic portrayals and cutesy animals, and I was hoping to attract people by such competitive advantage. Everyone I showed it to couldn't help but read the text and laugh at the whole thing, and they told me it truly captured my uniqueness, originality and charm. But then, something unexpected happened – when I took this photo for a test, and unlike I had hoped, it didn't influence my "likes" positively.

So, trying to find out what was going on, I took the original photo, sans the two thought bubbles, to *Photofeeler* (a website used to rate people's photos), and compared the two versions. The original photo scored an impressive 8.9/10, while the edited version, with the funny thinking animals, only had an average of 4.4/10. By trying to be funny and showing some real originality, my rating in "Smartness" lowered from 8.9 to 4.3; my "Trustworthiness" dropped from 8.3 to 3.7; and even my own "Attractiveness" fell from 9.4 to 5.2!

So, all things considered, not only does this prove even more what was discussed in previous chapters, but it also supports the idea that uniqueness and true originality are very negative assets in such places. It can all be synthesized like this – if I wanted to get "likes", I had to present people with the kind of content everyone is already showing them; but by truly being myself, I'd get few, if any, likes. And, from a realistic standpoint, this is profoundly hurtful, since it fosters a culture of unoriginality, falsity and idealism, where everyone looks the same, has the same dialogues time and again, and yet almost crazily seems to wish for a different outcome to the whole thing, time after time.

The idealistic "me" is currently very successful in online dating apps and websites – its profile has just three common photos and less than 10 words. The real "me" is someone few people ever talk to – its profile has six unique photos, and about 400 words which truly describe who I am. The person behind both is the exact same one, but it has to deny all of its originality to be able to talk to anyone in such places. The whole idea is as absurd as it sounds, and yet people continue living through it day after day, expecting a different outcome and supposedly not knowing what they're doing wrong (or they would fix it). It should, at the end of this whole thing, remind us all of a quote often but falsely attributed to Albert Einstein – "Insanity is doing the same thing over and over again and expecting different results."

	ID Photo (Algorithm 1 – Faceshape.com) 100 [%]	ID Photo (Algorithm 2 – facecomparison.toolpice.com) 79 [%]	ID Photo (Algorithm 3 – Faceplusplus.com) Very High [Probability]	ID Photo (Algorithm 4 – Facia.ai) 72 [%]	Probability of me being in the photo 72-100 [%]
Photo 1 (Backpack)	100	79	Very High	72	72-100
Photo 2 (Bookstore)	100	89	Very High	79	79-100
Photo 3 (Amphiteatre)	100	87	Very High	0	0-100
Photo 4 (Red Book)	100	91	Very High	75	75-100
Photo 5 (Greek Temple)	100	84	Very High	75	75-100
Photo 6 (Mediation)	100	90	Very High	79	79-100
Photo Taken Right Now	100	91	Very High	84	84-100
ID Photo	100	100	Very High	100	100-100
Photo Test1 (Ted with Beard)	0	7	Low	5	7
Photo Test2 (Ted without Beard)	0	6	Low	5	6

	AI Generated? (Algorithm 1 – isitai.com)	AI Generated? (Algorithm 2 – huggingface.co)	AI Generated? (Algorithm 3 – contentatscale.ai)	AI Generated? (Algorithm 4 – illuminarty.ai)	Probability of the photo being AI generated
Photo 1 (Backpack)	93 [%]	35 [%]	34 [%]	92 [%]	34-93 [%]
Photo 2 (Bookstore)	97	27	26	98	26-98
Photo 3 (Amphiteatre)	90	34	34	97	34-97
Photo 4 (Red Book)	98	79	79	5	5-98
Photo 5 (Greek Temple)	98	72	72	44	44-98
Photo 6 (Meditation)	13	45	44	3	3-45
Photo Taken Right Now	82	14	14	26	14-82
ID Photo	4	6	6	0	0-6
Photo Test1 (Ted with Beard)	60	5	5	17	5-60
Photo Test2 (Ted without Beard)	83	60	58	5	5-83